Books To Get High To

GET LOST IN THE WOODS

BY RYAN WASHINGTON

ISBN: 978-0692270493

For everyone who thought I was wasting my time, and for everyone who helped me waste it.

STOP

ENJOY

WHAT IS THIS, EXACTLY?

Books To Get High To
is your personal
gateway into a
dream-like state of
reflection, and
relaxation.

Sit down.
Light up.
Take off.

HOW DOES IT WORK?

STEP 1.
Select a quiet, relaxing setting.

STEP 2.
Get comfortable, and have your method of marijuana consumption ready.

STEP 3.
Suspend any skepticism to elevate your mind. Clear your head of any negative thoughts, and allow yourself to get lost.

BEFORE YOU BEGIN...

- A nice music playlist makes getting lost a little easier - unless you prefer silence.

- The text is only there to guide you, feel free to get lost all on your own. Make your own story.

- Don't rush. Make sure to spend as much time as you need on each page, and allow yourself to visualize your new surroundings.

- Explore. In this book, take yourself wherever you want to go.

TAKE

A

DEEP

BREATH

EMPTY YOUR MIND

FORGET WHERE YOU ARE

LET GO OF OF REALITY

Standing in a colorless land…

Immobilized by the absence of choice where everything is the same.

No path is more inviting than the next.

Decay is the only sound to be heard. Trees creak… leaves crumble.

A soft, silent wind carries with it a faint, but vivid memory.

You're reminded of something…

… so familiar.

It tries to find you, as your thoughts pour through a funnel…

… still on the tip of your tongue, and still not able to place it.

It's like a forgotten dream during the day,

slowly recreating itself, and then…

... you remember.

You're not sure if you've just entered a dream, or returned to reality.

It's a place where the only sound you hear is inspiration,

where extreme reality meets endless fantasy…

Life, chaotic and beautiful, surrounds you.

The trees stretch their roots, breathing heavily, quietly.

Every direction is asking to be explored…

… but again, immobilized, this time by the presence of choice.

Everything is just a moment ago.

The very recent past is presented constantly in the present.

Here, everything is déjà vu...

... blurring the difference between new, and familiar.

Forward is the only direction.

Deeper into the tall grass, the bushes, the trees…

Deeper into your wants, your needs…

... deeper into your dreams.

It's like everything you'd never say no to.

There's no going back...

Lose yourself here, to find yourself. The woods are endless…

… but the further you go,

the more fragile your perception becomes.

A careless step, and you find yourself in the middle…

… trapped…

… between your dreams, and what you think is reality.

It's impossible to tell one apart from the other.

Standing. Staring. Taking it all in.

A few last, deep breaths.

You allow yourself to let go.

One last look, a mental snapshot. You *can't* forget.

You want to remember this place when you go back…

… remember this feeling.

The color whispers goodbye as it gently slips away.

The memory, the sounds the smells, everything…

…faded.

You don't know if you are waking up, or falling asleep.

Back where you started,

waiting to remember that dream,

waiting to remember that reality…

… knowing that whatever it was, it's waiting for you too.

IT'S NOT OVER!

BOOKS TO GET HIGH TO
IS ONLY THE BEGINNING

YOU ARE NOW PART OF A COMMUNITY

STEP 1.

GO OUTSIDE

STEP 2.

TAKE PICTURES
OF YOUR FAVORITE SPOTS

STEP 3.

JOIN THE
BOOKS TO GET HIGH TO
COMMUNITY
ON YOUR FAVORITE SOCIAL MEDIA
APP

_____

TO SHARE YOUR PICTURES
TAG #BTGHT

www.ingramcontent.com/pod-product-compliance
Lightning Source LLC
Chambersburg PA
CBHW040231070426
42447CB00030B/96